FOR THE NEW CONVERT
NINE LESSONS

BY THE LATE
PASTOR R. ZENO GROCE

The publishing of this work was made possible by a gift of this manuscript from Pastor R. Zeno Groce to Pastor Jack Hicks. Both Pastors are with the Lord now.

All Scripture quotes are from
the King James Bible.

ISBN: 979-8-9877195-1-0

© Jack Hicks, May, 2013

Published February 2023

Cover design, formatting, and publishing by:
The Old Paths Publications, Inc.
Email: TOP@theoldpathspublications.com
Web address: www.theoldpathspublications.com

1.0

PREFACE

I feel that I wasted the first ten years of my Christian life simply because I didn't know what God wanted me to do. I spent three years in the Navy aboard the U.S.S. Massachusetts and with 2250 men I never witnessed to one soul. I didn't understand the Bible, and I was just the usual cold, unconcerned Christian.

When I was called to pastor a church, I felt the great need of instructing New Converts in the basic truths they would need to know in their new walk. I wanted every day of their Christian life to count for God.

This was the purpose of writing this book and with thousands already being used we trust many more will be used to help the new convert.

PASTOR R. ZENO GROCE
(Who has gone to his home in heaven.)

TABLE OF CONTENTS

TABLE OF CONTENTS

LESSON NO. 1

THE ASSURANCE OF SALVATION

Romans 8:16 The Spirit itself beareth witness with our spirit, that we are the children of God:

TIMES OF DOUBT:

One of the things the devil hounds every Christian with is the doubt of being saved. John the Baptist was a great preacher; he announced the coming of the Lord. He cried at His appearing, *"Behold the Lamb of God, which taketh away the sin of the world."* He baptized Jesus and heard the voice from heaven saying, "This is my Beloved Son, in whom I am well pleased." Yet while imprisoned, John began to doubt and sent his disciples to inquire of Jesus if He was the One or should they look for another.

THE NEED:

There will come times of doubting, and you will need something more than experience, visions, feelings or emotions to depend on. You can know that you are saved.

1. BECAUSE OF THE WORD:

> *1 John 5:13 These things have I written unto you that believe on the name of the Son of God; that ye may know that ye have eternal life, and that ye may believe on the name of the Son of God.*
>
> *Romans 10:9 That if thou shalt confess with thy mouth the Lord Jesus, and shalt believe in thine heart that God hath raised him from the dead, thou shalt be saved.*

2. BECAUSE OF THE LOVE FOR GOD'S PEOPLE:

> *1 John 3:14 We know that we have passed from death unto life, because we love the brethren. He that loveth not his brother abideth in death.*

There was a time in our lives when we only loved the person who loved us, and we weren't concerned about others; but when God saved us, He put a love within our hearts to love everybody. Even the people we at one time hated, now we love them.

Do you enjoy Christian Fellowship? Are you satisfied to be with God's people? Is there a love in your heart for the Christian? If so, it is good evidence you are saved.

3. BECAUSE OF THE HONOR FOR THE LORD'S COMMANDMENTS:

1 John 2:3 And hereby we do know that we know him, if we keep his commandments.

You don't have to make a real-born again person serve the Lord. The saved person obeys and serves the Lord through love.

The Lord commands us to live a separated life, to love and honor the church, to be soul-winners, to give of our means; and the person who has the new birth doesn't rebel against the commandments but strives to keep them.

4. BECAUSE OF DELIVERANCE FROM THE WORLD:

1 John 2:15 Love not the world, neither the things that are in the world. If any man love the world, the love of the Father is not in him.

I don't believe in sinless perfection, and I don't believe anyone lives above sin, but neither do I believe a born-again person enjoys sin.

> *2 Corinthians 5:17 Therefore if any man be in Christ, he is a new creature: old things are passed away; behold, all things are become new.*

It may be that a person in weakness would fall into a snare of the devil and do the wrong thing, but the Holy Spirit would make him conscious of his wrong, immediately.

5. BECAUSE OF TRUSTING IN JESUS:

> *John 1:11-12 He came unto his own, and his own received him not. But as many as received him, to them gave he power to become the sons of God, even to them that believe on his name:*

As best we know how, if we have put our trust in Jesus, nothing shall be able to separate us from Him.

A young boy, whom God had called to preach, was having a lot of trouble with doubt about his salvation. Finally, after much prayer and worry, he said" "I'm going to trust Jesus, if I die and go to hell." Then it dawned on him, if he trusted Jesus, he couldn't go to hell.

Do not put your faith in preachers, deacons, churches creeds, ordinances, rituals, ceremonies, sacraments or good works; just trust in Jesus.

LESSON NO. 2

WHAT THE CHURCH SHOULD MEAN TO YOU

Hebrews 10:25 Not forsaking the assembling of ourselves together, as the manner of some is; but exhorting one another: and so much the more, as ye see the day approaching.

THE EARLY CHURCH:

God, knowing this pilgrimage journey wouldn't be easy, led the early believers to establish a church whereby they might assemble together, pray, sing and preach, that they might be strong in the Lord. The Acts of the Apostles tell us of the trials and persecutions of this early church, but their gathering together always gave them new courage to go on.

GOOD ADVICE:

As a new convert, the best advice I could give you is to be faithful to the church and stay under the Word of God.

WHAT THE CHURCH SHOULD MEAN:

If you are saved, the Church should mean something to you. The person who boasts he can live just as good at home as he can at Church is not truthful, because if that were so, God would never have led the early Christians to organize the local Church.

1. THE CHURCH SHOULD BE A PLACE OF JOY:

Psalms 122:1 I was glad when they said unto me, Let us go into the house of the LORD.

2. THE CHURCH SHOULD BE A PLACE OF SPIRITUAL INSTRUCTION:

2 Timothy 2:15 Study to shew thyself approved unto God, a workman that needeth not to be ashamed, rightly dividing the word of truth.

Paul tells of God's gifts; of some prophets, some evangelists, some pastors and some teachers for the express purpose of the perfecting of the saints and edifying of the body of Christ.

You should belong to a Church that is sound in doctrine, and then be faithful to that Church and stay under the teaching of the sound doctrine, so that you can be stedfast in the Word without wavering and being tossed about with every wind of doctrine.

I have seen new converts start running after everything that comes along, and before long they did not know what they believed.

3. IT SHOULD BE A PLACE OF PERSONAL INTEREST:

2 Samuel 7:2 That the king said unto Nathan the prophet, See now, I dwell in an house of cedar, but the ark of God dwelleth within curtains.

David realized he lived in a beautiful house, and all his interest had been there, while the ark of God dwelt in a tent.

We should have a personal interest in the Church and desire to keep it the most beautiful building in the community.

4. IT SHOULD BE A PLACE OF

HONOR AND PRAISE:

Philippians 2:3 Let nothing be done through strife or vainglory; but in lowliness of mind let each esteem other better than themselves.

Instead of running down the Church and the people, Paul said we should esteem our brothers. Our Church should be a place of high esteem, and instead of criticizing people in it, we should love and pray for them.

The reason sinners have no respect for the Church, is because the members are always running down the Church.

THE SIN OF MISSING CHURCH:

If, after God has saved us and we are baptized into the fellowship of the Church, we are not faithful and stay away from Church, we have sinned against God and broken the vows we made.

1. THE SIN OF DISOBEDIENCE TO GOD'S COMMAND:

Hebrews 10:25 Not forsaking the assembling of ourselves together, as the manner of some is; but exhorting one another: and so much the more, as ye see the day approaching.

God has commanded us to assemble together, and if we fail to attend Church, we sin against God's commandments:

2. THE SIN OF NEGLECTING OUR CHILDREN:

Ephesians 6:4 And, ye fathers, provoke not your children to wrath: but bring them up in the nurture and admonition of the Lord.

As the parent of the child, it's your duty to bring that child to Church. To neglect the Church is to neglect your child.

3. THE SIN OF FAILING TO GROW IN GRACE AND KNOWLEDGE:

2 Peter 3:18 But grow in grace, and in the knowledge of our Lord and Saviour Jesus Christ. To him be glory both now and for ever. Amen.

Those who fail to attend Church

will no doubt neglect studying God's Word. The great sin of many Church members is that they know nothing of the Word of God.

LESSON NO. 3

THE WAY TO BE HAPPY AND PLEASE GOD

Matthew 7:28-29 And it came to pass, when Jesus had ended these sayings, the people were astonished at his doctrine: For he taught them as one having authority, and not as the scribes.

SEARCH FOR HAPPINESS:

The world is always searching for happiness. They are looking for a thrill. Yet the only people who can be truly happy are Christians, and then, Christians can only be happy when they obey the Lord. There is a way for the saved person to be happy and please God.

USE SCRIPTURE:

The Scripture used from the Book of Matthew is recognized as the *"Sermon on the Mount."* Jesus took His disciples aside into the mountain and told them how to live as Christians and how to be happy. When He finished, they were astonished and admitted that He spoke with authority.

WHAT JESUS TAUGHT THEM:

If Jesus felt the need to teach His followers these truths, then we need to sit at His feet and learn the same.

1. HE TAUGHT THEM THE SECRET OF HAPPINESS:

Matthew 5:2-11 And he opened his mouth, and taught them, saying, Blessed are the poor in spirit: for theirs is the kingdom of heaven. Blessed are they that mourn: for they shall be comforted. Blessed are the meek: for they shall inherit the earth. Blessed are they which do hunger and thirst after righteousness: for they shall be filled. Blessed are the merciful: for they shall obtain mercy. Blessed are the pure in heart: for they shall see God. Blessed are the peacemakers: for they shall be called the children of God. Blessed are they which are persecuted for righteousness' sake: for theirs is the kingdom of heaven. Blessed are ye, when men shall revile you, and persecute you, and shall say all manner of evil against you falsely, for my sake.

Jesus taught the followers that true happiness did not consist of the material possessions in this life, but rather in our threefold attitude; our attitude toward God, our attitude toward our fellowman and our attitude toward ourself.

The person that doesn't have a penny in the world can be the happiest person by possession of the characteristics Jesus declares.

2. HE TAUGHT THEM THE POWER OF INFLUENCE:

Matthew 5:16 "Let your light so shine before men, that they may see your good works, and glorify your Father which is in heaven.

Jesus taught His followers that they were to be the light to those who believed not, and that by their behavior, the world would judge the worth of following Christ.

The only thing the world knows about Christianity, the Bible or the

Church, is in the lives of those who profess to be saved. Our lives are living Epistles to this world, and what we do, say or where we go influences the unbeliever one way or the other. We should let the beauty of Jesus be seen in us at all times.

3. HE TAUGHT THEM THE DIRECTIONS FOR PRAYER:

Matthew 6:6 But thou, when thou prayest, enter into thy closet, and when thou hast shut thy door, pray to thy Father which is in secret; and thy Father which seeth in secret shall reward thee openly.

These followers who had seen the Pharisees pray on the street corner, making long prayers to be seen of men, learned that such was not the way to reach the throne of Grace, but to close out the world and pray to the Father.

The secret of prayer is not how loud or how long we can pray, but with a sincere heart talk to God as if we were talking to our earthly father.

4. HE TAUGHT THEM THE MOST PROFITABLE INVESTMENT:

Matthew 6:20 But lay up for

yourselves treasures in heaven, where neither moth nor rust doth corrupt, and where thieves do not break through nor steal:

The disciples had left all to follow Jesus, but he taught them that the things of this life will decay and fade away, but the treasure we lay up in heaven will be for eternity.

The only thing that will ever count when this life is over will be what we have done for God.

The story is told of the old lady who wanted to go on, because all she had was in Heaven. She said the Lord took her preacher husband some years ago. During the thirty years she and her husband served on the mission field, they did all their banking in Heaven. They invested all their money in the Lord's work. All the folks she grew up with had gone on to be with the Lord. She said "All I have is on the other side and I want to go on."

5. HE TAUGHT THEM THE FATHER'S CARE FOR HIS OWN:

Matthew 6:26 Behold the fowls of the air: for they sow not, neither do they reap, nor gather into barns; yet your heavenly Father feedeth them. Are ye not much better than they?

These followers probably wondered at times where the next meal was coming from, or where their clothes would come from, but Jesus told them that the Father would take care of his own.

Instead of worrying ourselves to death about how we are going to make it, we need to learn how God cares for his own.

Psalms 37:25 I have been young, and now am old; yet have I not seen the righteous forsaken, nor his seed begging bread.

Said the Robin to the Sparrow,
I would really like to know
Why these anxious human beings
Rush about and hurry so.

Said the Sparrow to the Robin,
Friend, I think that it must be
That they have no Heavenly Father
Such as cares for you and me.

LESSON NO. 4

WHAT SIN DOES TO A CHRISTIAN

1 Corinthians 6:19-20 What? know ye not that your body is the temple of the Holy Ghost which is in you, which ye have of God, and ye are not your own? For ye are bought with a price: therefore glorify God in your body, and in your spirit, which are God's.

THE CHRISTIAN'S RELATIONSHIP WITH GOD:

When a person is saved, they are born into the family of God. No longer do they belong to the devil, but now their name is written in heaven and they belong to God. So many Christians take this relationship with God so lightly, but God does not count it lightly. Being in the family of God our acts and deeds are accountable to God.

SIN IN A CHRISTIAN'S LIFE:

Up to the time we were saved, our

acts and deeds were our own business, but now we are not our own, we have been bought with a price; and if we let sin come in our life as a Christian, it will cost.

1. SIN SEPARATES US FROM THE FELLOWSHIP OF GOD:

Isaiah 59:2 But your iniquities have separated between you and your God, and your sins have hid his face from you, that he will not hear.

The first thing sin does in a Christian's life is separate us from the fellowship of God. God is a Holy God and will not look upon sin, therefore, because of our sin, God turns His face away.

When the fellowship is broken we can pray, but there is no answer. We can read the Bible but it has no meaning and freshness.

Psalms 66:18 If I regard iniquity in my heart, the Lord will not hear me:

2. SIN WILL DESTROY THE JOY OF SALVATION:

David was a man 'after God's own heart'; he enjoyed the presence of the

Lord and God blessed him mightily until sin destroyed that joy; and David wept with grief, desiring to have the joy again.

> *Psalms 51:12 Restore unto me the joy of thy salvation; and uphold me with thy free spirit.*

The second phase of sin in a Christian's life is the lost joy of salvation. The joy of going to Church, the joy of testifying, the joy of seeing souls saved. When you reach this state you begin to find fault with everything and everyone.

3. SIN WILL BRING THE CHASTENING HAND OF GOD:

> *Hebrews 12:6 For whom the Lord loveth he chasteneth, and scourgeth every son whom he receiveth.*

The third state of sin in a Christian's life is the chastening hand of God. God the Father is forced to whip us because of our disobedience and unwillingness to confess our sin.

This chastening may be in sickness; it may be disappointments, it may be financial loss, it may be troubles upon troubles, but God will chasten us for sin.

4. SIN CAUSES GOD TO TAKE AWAY THE PRECIOUS THINGS:

Because of David's sin, God took the most precious thing he had; the child that was born.

2 Samuel 12:14 Howbeit, because by this deed thou hast given great occasion to the enemies of the LORD to blaspheme, the child also that is born unto thee shall surely die.

A saved person that turns away from God into sin and refuses to repent of that sin even after the chastening hand of God is upon them, is headed for great sorrow. If necessary God will take from us the precious things in order to bring us back to Him.

I have heard one of our members tell many times how he turned away from God, quit going to church and God took two of his children before he repented and turned back to God.

5. SIN CAN BRING PREMATURE DEATH:

The fifth and most serious state of sin is when God's patience is exhausted and He turns you over to the devil for the destruction of the flesh.

> *1 Corinthians 5:5 To deliver such an one unto Satan for the destruction of the flesh, that the spirit may be saved in the day of the Lord Jesus.*

> *1 John 5:16 If any man see his brother sin a sin which is not unto death, he shall ask, and he shall give him life for them that sin not unto death. There is a sin unto death: I do not say that he shall pray for it.*

If a person is determined not to mind God and repent not at the chastening hand of God, and continues on in sin, then there will come a time when God signs their death warrant and they will fill a premature grave.

6. THE SOLUTION TO SIN IN A CHRISTIAN'S LIFE:

> *1 John 1:9 If we confess our sins, he is faithful and just to forgive us our sins, and to cleanse us from all unrighteousness.*

LESSON NO. 5

GIVING THE BIBLE WAY

Leviticus 27:30 And all the tithe of the land, whether of the seed of the land, or of the fruit of the tree, is the LORD'S: it is holy unto the LORD.

QUESTION:

One of the questions in the mind of every new convert is how to give, how much to give, where to give and when to give.

ANSWER:

The answer to these questions are found in the Bible. The storehouse is the church. A tithe is a tenth and the way will be covered later in the lesson.

THE BLESSING:

The Bible says there is a blessing in tithing. The promise is that if we will bring our tithe to the storehouse, God will open the windows of heaven and pour us out a blessing that we can't contain. One of the teachers in our church said someone made the statement to him that they couldn't afford to tithe. He replied to them that he couldn't afford not to tithe.

GIVING THE BIBLE WAY:

1. ABRAHAM STARTED IT:

Some say that tithing is under the law, but long before the law was given Abraham had been to deliver his nephew Lot from the enemy and was returning when Melchizedek, king of Salem, met him. Melchizedek was the priest of the most high God and a type of Jesus. The Word says Abraham gave tithes of all.

> *Genesis 14:18-20 And Melchizedek king of Salem brought forth bread and wine: and he was the priest of the most high God. And he blessed him, and said, Blessed be Abram of the most high God, possessor of heaven and earth: And blessed be the most high God, which hath delivered thine enemies into thy hand. And he gave him tithes of all.*

2. JACOB CONTINUED IT:

After Jacob had the vision of the heavenly ladder, he awoke, and said "Surely the Lord is in this place:" and he placed a stone at the place and called it "Bethel." There Jacob made a vow to God.

> *Genesis 28:20-22 And Jacob vowed a vow, saying, If God will be with me, and will keep me in this way that I go, and will give me bread to eat, and raiment to put on, So that I come again to my father's house in peace; then shall the LORD be my God: And this stone, which I have set for a pillar, shall be God's house: and of all that thou shalt give me I will surely give the tenth unto thee.*

3. MOSES INCORPORATED IT:

After the law was given to Moses, God called him back to the mountain to give him directions for building the tabernacle, a place where God could meet with man. For the building and support of the tabernacle God commanded that the people give a tenth of all they had and Moses incorporated this commandment into the law.

Leviticus 27:30 And all the tithe of

the land, whether of the seed of the land, or of the fruit of the tree, is the LORD'S: it is holy unto the LORD.

4. MALACHI COMMANDED IT:

Malachi is telling God's people to return to the Lord and he asks the question, "Will a man rob God?" and then says that a man robs God in tithes and offerings. Then Malachi commands them to tithe.

Malachi 3:10 Bring ye all the tithes into the storehouse, that there may be meat in mine house, and prove me now herewith, saith the LORD of hosts, if I will not open you the windows of heaven, and pour you out a blessing, that there shall not be room enough to receive it.

5. JESUS COMMENDED IT:

Jesus was denouncing the Scribes and Pharisees for their religious acts that had no depth. He accused them of outward acts but no inward truth. He said they had done some of the things but left undone weightier matters. Jesus makes it clear that while there are more important things we should never leave tithing out.

Matthew 23:23 Woe unto you, scribes and Pharisees, hypocrites! for ye pay tithe of mint and anise and cummin, and have omitted the weightier matters of the law, judgment, mercy, and faith: these ought ye to have done, and not to leave the other undone.

6. GOD ORDAINED IT:

Paul, writing to the church of Corinth, was telling them that they should support the work of spreading the gospel, because God had ordained it that way.

1 Corinthians 9:14 Even so hath the Lord ordained that they which preach the gospel should live of the gospel.

7. PAUL EXPLAINED IT:

As Paul continues his letter to the Corinthians, he explains the way to give and when to give.

1 Corinthians 16:2 Upon the first day of the week let every one of you lay by him in store, as God hath prospered him, that there be no gatherings when I come.

LESSON NO. 6

ORDINANCES OF THE CHURCH

Colossians 1:8 Who also declared unto us your love in the Spirit.

There are only two ordinances in a Baptist Church. One is Baptism and the other The Lord's Supper. Both ordinances are very sacred and are regarded as such by our church. Both ordinances are the symbol of the death, burial, and resurrection of our Lord and Saviour.

ORDINANCES:

THIS LESSON:

The purpose of this lesson is to acquaint you with the meaning of these ordinances that you might grow in Grace and Knowledge.

1. BAPTISM:

Baptism is an open and public profession of faith in Christ our Saviour. The new convert goes down into a watery grave, picturing the burial of

Christ and picturing his own death to sin, the crucifixion of the natural man, and rises to walk in the newness of life.

TWO ERRORS IN REGARD TO BAPTISM:

1. THAT ONE CANNOT BE SAVED WITHOUT BAPTISM:

To say we are saved by baptism is to say salvation is by works. If it is works, it leaves out grace and the Word teaches, we are saved by grace.

Ephesians 2:8-9 For by grace are ye saved through faith; and that not of yourselves: it is the gift of God: Not of works, lest any man should boast.

It is clear in the Bible that people believed first, and then were baptized.

2. THAT BAPTISM IS NOT IMPORTANT:

Although baptism is not essential to Salvation it is important that every Christian be baptized and the Bible declares why:

JESUS WAS BAPTIZED:

Matthew 3:13 Then cometh

Jesus from Galilee to Jordan unto John, to be baptized of him.

JESUS COMMANDS US TO BE BAPTIZED:

Matthew 28:19 Go ye therefore, and teach all nations, baptizing them in the name of the Father, and of the Son, and of the Holy Ghost:

THE CONVERTS OF THE EARLY CHURCH WERE BAPTIZED:

THE ETHIOPIAN EUNUCH:

Acts 8:38 And he commanded the chariot to stand still: and they went down both into the water, both Philip and the eunuch; and he baptized him.

PAUL, THE APOSTLE:

Acts 9:18 And immediately there fell from his eyes as it had been scales: and he received sight forthwith, and arose, and was baptized.

CORNELIUS AND HIS HOUSEHOLD:

Acts 10:48 And he commanded them to be baptized in the name of the Lord. Then prayed they him to tarry certain days.

LYDIA:

Acts 16:15 And when she was baptized, and her household, she besought us, saying, If ye have judged me to be faithful to the Lord, come into my house, and abide there. And she constrained us.

THE PHILIPPIAN JAILER:

Acts 16:33 And he took them the same hour of the night, and washed their stripes; and was baptized, he and all his, straightway.

FORM OF BAPTISM:

There are many different opinions as to the form of baptism, but let us look into the Word and see what the Bible says:

1. REQUIRES WATER:

John 1:26 John answered them, saying, I baptize with water: but there standeth one among you, whom ye know not;

2. REQUIRES MUCH WATER:

John 3:23 And John also was baptizing in Aenon near to Salim, because there was much water there: and they came, and were baptized.

3. REQUIRES GOING DOWN INTO THE WATER:

Acts 8:38 And he commanded the chariot to stand still: and they went down both into the water, both Philip and the eunuch; and he baptized him.

4. REQUIRES BURIAL IN WATER:

Romans 6:4 Therefore we are buried with him by baptism into death: that like as Christ was raised up from the dead by the glory of the Father, even so we also should walk in newness of life.

5. REQUIRES RESURRECTION FROM THE WATER:

Matthew 3:16 And Jesus, when he was baptized, went up straightway out of the water: and, lo, the heavens were opened unto him, and he saw the Spirit of God descending like a dove, and lighting upon him:

THE LORD'S SUPPER:

We come now to observe the

Lord's Supper, the most sacred service we can observe, This is a time when our very soul is drawn close to the Lord; a time when we should humbly repent of the sin in our life and turn to the cross.

QUESTIONS CONCERNING THE LORD'S SUPPER:

1. WHY DO WE OBSERVE THE LORD'S SUPPER?

1 Corinthians 11:26 For as often as ye eat this bread, and drink this cup, ye do shew the Lord's death till he come.

2. WHO IS ELIGIBLE TO RECEIVE COMMUNION:

1 Corinthians 11:28 But let a man examine himself, and so let him eat of that bread, and drink of that cup.

3. WHAT DOES THE BREAD REPRESENT?

1 Corinthians 11:24 And when he had given thanks, he brake it, and said, Take, eat: this is my body, which is broken for you: this do in remembrance of me.

4. WHAT DOES THE CUP REPRESENT?

1 Corinthians 11:25 After the same manner also he took the cup, when he had supped, saying, This cup is the new testament in my blood: this do ye, as oft as ye drink it, in remembrance of me.

5. HOW OFTEN SHOULD WE OBSERVE THE LORD'S SUPPER?

Some churches observe the supper every Sunday, some every month, some each quarter, some once each year. The Bible doesn't give a set time but only says *"as oft as you do."*

LESSON NO. 7

THE SECOND COMING

John 14:1-3 Let not your heart be troubled: ye believe in God, believe also in me. In my Father's house are many mansions: if it were not so, I would have told you. I go to prepare a place for you. And if I go and prepare a place for you, I will come again, and receive you unto myself; that where I am, there ye may be also.

THREE REASONS FOR TEACHING THE SECOND COMING:

1. BECAUSE IT IS THE NEXT IMPORTANT STEP IN GOD'S CALENDAR OF EVENTS:

- The first event was His birth.
- The second and greatest of all, His death.
- The third was His bodily resurrection.
- The fourth was His ascending

43

back to Heaven.

➢ **The next will be His return.**

2. BECAUSE THE MAJORITY KNOW NOTHING ABOUT THIS GREAT EVENT:

The average Christian of today knows very little if anything about the second coming of Christ, and to many who are leaders in the church, it is a strange doctrine.

3. BECAUSE IT CAUSES THE CHRISTIAN TO BE READY:

The Christian that is looking for Jesus to come any moment will live a separated and holy life.

> *1 John 3:2-3 Beloved, now are we the sons of God, and it doth not yet appear what we shall be: but we know that, when he shall appear, we shall be like him; for we shall see him as he is. And every man that hath this hope in him purifieth himself, even as he is pure.*

THE SIGN OF HIS COMING:

> *Matthew 24:3 And as he sat upon the mount of Olives, the disciples came unto him privately, saying,*

Tell us, when shall these things be? and what shall be the sign of thy coming, and of the end of the world?

While Jesus told them not to look for a sign, but to always be ready, He did reveal unto them some of the things that would come to pass in the last days before His coming again.

THREE MAJOR SIGNS:

While there are a number of other signs, I want to use the three major ones that point to the immediate coming of our Lord.

1. MORAL SITUATION:

Matthew 24:37-38 But as the days of Noe were, so shall also the coming of the Son of man be. For as in the days that were before the flood they were eating and drinking, marrying and giving in marriage, until the day that Noe entered into the ark,

Jesus was saying that the moral condition of the world will return similar to the days of Noah. All the things that Jesus mentions of the days of Noah are prevalent on every hand today. The drinking problem is out of control, marriage vows mean nothing and the moral condition is at the lowest state.

2. RELIGIOUS SITUATION:

2 Timothy 3:1, 5 This know also, that in the last days perilous times shall come. Having a form of godliness, but denying the power thereof: from such turn away.

More churches are being built today, more people are joining the churches than ever before and religion is very popular, yet the spiritual condition of our world is dark. The reason is revealed in this Scripture. Religions today have a form of godliness, but deny the power of God.

3. JEWISH SITUATION:

Luke 21:29-30 And he spake to them a parable; Behold the fig tree, and all the trees; When they now shoot forth, ye see and know of your own selves that summer is now nigh at hand.

The fig tree has always been the symbol of the Jews and the Jews are God's time clock, and anything happening involving the Jew is a mark of time.

WHAT WILL HAPPEN WHEN JESUS COMES:

1 Thessalonians 4:16-17 For the Lord himself shall descend from heaven with a shout, with the voice of the archangel, and with the trump of God: and the dead in Christ shall rise first: Then we which are alive and remain shall be caught up together with them in the clouds, to meet the Lord in the air: and so shall we ever be with the Lord.

1. THE CHRISTIANS WHO HAVE FALLEN ASLEEP WILL RISE FIRST:

The soul and spirit has been separated from the body by death.

2 Corinthians 5:8 We are confident, I say, and willing rather to be absent from the body, and to be present with the Lord.

Now the body comes forth from the grave and is reunited with soul and spirit and changed into a glorified body.

2. THE CHRISTIANS WHO ARE STILL LIVING WILL BE CAUGHT UP:

The Christians who are still living when Jesus comes will be caught up to meet the Lord in the clouds.

3. THE LOST PERSON WHO HAS DIED WILL REMAIN THE SAME:

That lost man or woman's body remains in the grave and their soul and spirit in hell until the "White Throne Judgment."

> *Revelation 20:5 But the rest of the dead lived not again until the thousand years were finished. This is the first resurrection.*

4. THE LOST PERSON WHO IS LIVING WILL BE LEFT HERE:

The lost person place, who is living will be left here when the rapture takes place.

> *Matthew 24:40-41 Then shall two be in the field; the one shall be taken, and the other left. Two women shall be grinding at the mill; the one shall be taken, and the other left.*

JUDGMENT SEAT OF CHRIST:

2 Corinthians 5:10 For we must all appear before the judgment seat of Christ; that every one may receive the things done in his body, according to that he hath done, whether it be good or bad.

1. TAKES PLACE JUST AFTER THE RAPTURE:

This judgment takes place just after the church has been caught away to be with the Lord.

2. EVERY CHILD OF GOD SHALL APPEAR:

This judgment is for the Christian and every child of God shall appear.

3. JUDGMENT OF OUR WORKS:

This is not a judgment as to our sin; our sins were judged at Calvary and when we received Jesus that was settled, but from the day we are saved until this time, we will be judged according to what we have done for God, and the use of the talents he has given us.

MARRIAGE SUPPER:

Revelation 19:7-9 Let us be glad and rejoice, and give honour to him: for the marriage of the Lamb is come, and his wife hath made herself ready. And to her was granted that she should be arrayed in fine linen, clean and white: for the fine linen is the righteousness of saints. And he saith unto me, Write, Blessed are they which are called unto the marriage supper of the Lamb. And he saith unto me, These are the true sayings of God.

The marriage supper will be a glorious occasion and those present shall rejoice.

1. THE BRIDEGROOM:

Jesus, the bridegroom will be present.

2. BRIDE:

The bride, the church will be present.

3. THE INVITED:

The invited guests will be the Old Testament saints.

TRIBULATION:

Matthew 24:21 For then shall be great tribulation, such as was not since the beginning of the world to this time, no, nor ever shall be.

While the church spends the seven years with the Lord in the sky. those who are left upon the earth will face the tribulation period.

1. THE THREE UNHOLY PERSONS:

(a) Dragon: (The devil will rule with great power during this time)

(b) Beast: (The Anti-Christ who will be a Gentile ruler with great, great wonders)

(c) False Prophet: (Religious leader)

2. GOD'S WRATH:

(a) Seven Seals: (War, famine, death, earthquake, sun and moon blackened)

(b) Seven trumpets: (Hail, fire, mingled blood, wormwood, scorpions of death)

(c) Seven vials: (Grievous sores, water to blood, scorching sun)

BATTLE OF ARMAGEDDON:

Revelation 16:16 And he gathered them together into a place called in the Hebrew tongue Armageddon.

At the close of the tribulation Satan has gathered the armies of the earth around Jerusalem to destroy the Jews.

1. THE PLACE OF THE BATTLE:

In the valley just north of Jerusalem.

2. THE PARTICIPANTS:

The Jew will not engage in the battle, for Christ will return with mighty power and destroy the armies with the sword from his mouth. Blood then will run through the valley as high as the horses bridle.

3. THE RESULTS:

Christ is victorious.

JUDGMENT OF THE NATIONS:

Matthew 25:31-32 When the Son

of man shall come in his glory, and all the holy angels with him, then shall he sit upon the throne of his glory: And before him shall be gathered all nations: and he shall separate them one from another, as a shepherd divideth his sheep from the goats:

This is the judgment for those who are left upon the earth after the tribulation and after the battle of Armageddon.

1. SHEEP:

The Jews who have been preserved, the Jews who have now believed and the Gentiles who have believed the preaching of the Jews.

2. GOATS:

The sinners who have rejected the Word of God during this period. At this time some shall cry and say "Lord, Lord did we not do many things."

THE MILLENNIUM:

Revelation 20:6 Blessed and holy is he that hath part in the first resurrection: on such the second death hath no power, but they shall be priests of God and of

Christ, and shall reign with him a thousand years.

This period follows the judgment of the nations and seven important things will happen during this time.

1. Satan will be chained.
2. Ferociousness of the beast will vanish.
3. Wars will be no more.
4. Knowledge of the Lord will cover the earth.
5. Curse on the earth will be removed.
6. Jesus will rule the earth.
7. The Saints will rule and reign with Christ.

SATAN'S LAST STAND:

Revelation 20:7-8 And when the thousand years are expired, Satan shall be loosed out of his prison, And shall go out to deceive the nations which are in the four quarters of the earth, Gog and Magog, to gather them together to battle: the number of whom is as the sand of the sea.

When Satan is loosed he will deceive the children born to the people who enter the millennium as humans. During the thousand years many shall be born and death will not be, so they shall be as the sand of the sea in number. When Satan gathers this host together to destroy Christ, fire comes from heaven and consumes the host and Satan is cast into the lake of fire with the beast and the beast and the false prophet.

Revelation 20:10 And the devil that deceived them was cast into the lake of fire and brimstone, where the beast and the false prophet are, and shall be tormented day and night for ever and ever.

THE WHITE THRONE JUDGMENT:

Revelation 20:11 And I saw a great white throne, and him that sat on it, from whose face the earth and the heaven fled away; and there was found no place for them.

HEAVEN:

Revelation 21:1-2 And I saw a new heaven and a new earth: for the first heaven and the first earth were passed away; and there was no more sea. And I John saw the holy city, new Jerusalem, coming down from God out of heaven, prepared as a bride adorned for her husband.

SEVEN NEW THINGS:

1. New Heaven:
2. New Earth:
3. New Jerusalem:
4. New Tabernacle:
5. New People:
6. New Light:
7. New Paradise:

SEVEN NO MORES:

1. No More Sea:
2. No More Death:
3. No More Sorrow:
4. No More Crying:
5. No More Pain:
6. No More Curse:
7. No More Night:

LESSON NO. 8

THE CHURCH COVENANT

Acts 2:41-47 Then they that gladly received his word were baptized: and the same day there were added unto them about three thousand souls. And they continued stedfastly in the apostles' doctrine and fellowship, and in breaking of bread, and in prayers. And fear came upon every soul: and many wonders and signs were done by the apostles. And all that believed were together, and had all things common; And sold their possessions and goods, and parted them to all men, as every man had need. And they, continuing daily with one accord in the temple, and breaking bread from house to house, did eat their meat with gladness and singleness of heart, Praising God, and having favour with all the people. And the Lord added to the church daily such as should be saved.

CHURCH MEMBERSHIP:

To be saved is one thing and to join the church is another. We are careful to separate the invitations because we don't want anyone to think you are saved by joining the church. The one qualification of church membership is to be saved.

SERIOUSNESS OF CHURCH MEMBERSHIP:

Every saved person should join the church and be baptized and this lesson is to help you understand what you do when you join.

THE CHURCH COVENANT:

Having been led, as we believe, by the Spirit of God, to receive the Lord Jesus Christ as our Saviour, and on the profession of our faith, having been baptized in the name of the Father, and of the Son, and of the Holy Ghost, we do now, (1) in the presence of God, Angels and this assembly, most solemnly and joyfully enter into this covenant with one another, as one body in Christ.

We engage, therefore, by the aid of the Holy Spirit, to (1) walk together in Christian love; to (2) strive for the advancement of this church, in knowledge, holiness and comfort; to (3) promote its prosperity and spirituality; to (4) sustain its worship, ordinances, discipline, and doctrines; to (5) contribute cheerfully and regularly to the support of the ministry, the expense of the church, the relief of the poor, and the spread of the Gospel through all nations. We also engage to (1) maintain family and secret devotions; to (2) religiously educate our children; to (3) seek the salvation of our kindred and acquaintances; to (4) walk circumspectly in the world; to be just in our dealings, faithful in our engagements and exemplary in our deportment, to (5) avoid all tattling, backbiting, and excessive anger; to (6) abstain from the sale and use of intoxicating drink as a beverage, and to (7) be zealous in our efforts to advance the kingdom of our Saviour.

We further engage to (1) watch over one another in brotherly love; to (2) remember each other in prayer; to (3) aid each other in sickness and distress; to (4) cultivate Christian sympathy in feeling and courtesy in speech, to (5) be slow to take offense, but always ready for reconciliation and (6) mindful of the rules of our Saviour, to secure it without delay.

We moreover engage that, (1) when we remove from this place, we will as soon as possible unite with some other church where we can carry out the spirit of this covenant and the principles of God's Word.

LESSON NO. 9

HOW TO BE A SOUL WINNER

Proverbs 11:30 The fruit of the righteous is a tree of life; and he that winneth souls is wise.

BUSINESS OF SOUL WINNING:

The business of winning souls is the greatest business on earth. The greatest joy beyond being saved yourself is winning someone else to Christ. The greatest thing about this business is that everyone can be a soul winner. Some of the greatest soul winners have been men and women who are timid, handicapped, uneducated and lacking in personality.

THE A.B.C's OF SOUL WINNING:

To help us to understand this business of soul winning, let us consider the simple A.B.C's of this matter.

1. (A) APPEARANCE:

Appearance is an all-important factor in this business of winning souls to Christ. The unconverted person has all kind of strange ideas about Christians, therefore, we should represent our Lord Jesus in the very best way we can. We should dress up in our very best for this task. We should be careful that nothing about us would offend the person we are trying to win to Christ.

2. (B) BEHAVIOR:

When you arrive at the home or place of your prospect there are some things to be mindful of. Be nice to that prospect no matter what condition they might be in or what manner they may be dressed. If their response to your visit is unpleasant we must be nice.

Second be careful about going in. There are certain times when it would be better to excuse yourself and tell the prospect you will come back.

Third be complimentary when you are invited in. You must win the confidence of your prospect before you can win them to Christ.

Finally be sure to talk of things that interest your prospect so they will start talking and answer you when the all-important question is asked.

3. (C) COMPASSION:

You will never be a successful soul winner until you possess a deep compassion for souls. You must be mindful that the person you talk to is a living soul, and will live forever either in heaven or hell, and what you say or do could make the difference. Prayer must precede every visit. Praying for the Holy Spirit to direct you, and praying that He will prepare the prospect, going with compassion and using the Word of God as the Seed, we have the promise that we shall reach souls.

THE QUESTION:

As soon as you can, and as God leads, come to the question about their relationship with God. Two questions are sufficient.

1. The First Question is this: "ARE YOU A CHRISTIAN?"

Listen carefully for the answer as this will reveal their relationship with the Lord. If they should answer "no" then you can proceed with the Word in showing them how they can be saved. If they give you a good firm answer of knowing they are saved, then you can have prayer with them, but if they answer with such phrases as "I think I am." or "I do the best I know how," or "I joined the church and go when I can," then you know they are not saved and you can present the second question.

2. The Second Question is this: "IF YOU DIED TODAY WOULD YOU KNOW YOU WOULD GO TO HEAVEN?"

Unless they are truly born again they cannot answer this question with sincerity. When they reply "I don't believe anyone could say that," then you say "would you let me show you from the Bible how you can know?" Whatever way they may answer the second question you can lead them to the Word at that time.

USING THE NEW TESTAMENT:

When the time comes to use the Testament then be ready with the Testament marked. Begin with these words: "there are three important things that God wants everyone to know, therefore He has made it very clear in His Word."

1. EVERYONE NEEDS TO KNOW THEY ARE A SINNER:

Romans 3:23 For all have sinned, and come short of the glory of God;

Explain that God set a standard and that standard was His Glory and we have all come short of that standard. Do not condemn your prospect but include yourself and any other person with you. You might call the prospect by name and say "this places all of us in the same category, we are all born sinners."

2. EVERYONE NEEDS TO KNOW THEY MUST BE BORN AGAIN:

John 3:3 Jesus answered and said unto him, Verily, verily, I say unto thee, Except a man be born again, he cannot see the kingdom of God.

3. EVERYONE NEEDS TO KNOW THEY CAN BE SAVED:

Revelation 3:20 Behold, I stand at the door, and knock: if any man hear my voice, and open the door, I will come in to him, and will sup with him, and he with me.

Explain to your prospect that Christ

is knocking at their heart's door and He wants to come in, but the door must be opened by them.

4. THIS IS YOUR FINAL QUESTION:

"Would you be willing to bow your head right now and ask the Lord to save you?" Pray with them and for them.

ABOUT THE AUTHOR

(This information was retrieved from his obituary.)

Pastor Zeno Groce June 22, 1922 - Dec. 10, 2012, a faithful Minister of the Gospel, went to be with his Lord on December 10, 2012 surrounded by his loving family. Zeno gave his life serving others and was pastor of Woodland Baptist Church for 46 years until his retirement in 1998. He was born in Yadkin County on June 22, 1922 to Daniel Webster Groce and Emma Rutledge Groce. Zeno met Helen Hicks and they were married on April 3, 1942 and the couple was blessed with three sons. On September 1, 1942 he enlisted in the US Navy and began active duty aboard the U.S.S. Massachusetts during World War II. After receiving his honorable discharge in October 1945, he worked for Parrish Tire Company for 11 years. In the summer of 1953 Zeno felt the call of God on his life to be a minister of the Gospel and was ordained as pastor of Woodland Baptist Church on April 24, 1955. During his 46 years as pastor, the congregation grew from 100 in attendance to as high as 2,000. Zeno preached at revival services throughout the southeast and served as a mentor to numbers of pastors. In addition to his parents, he was preceded in death by his son, Danny in 2009, all of his siblings, Howard, Buford "Skeet", Mamie Rhodes, Adelene Rhodes and Ruby Foster. He is survived by his loving wife of over 70 years, Helen, two sons; Mike (Brenda) Groce of Newton, and Joel (Donna) Groce of Winston-Salem; a daughter-in-law, Pam Groce of Rural Hall; three grandchildren, Michele (Gregg) Gibson of Maiden, Brian (Gwen) Groce of Campobello, SC, and Amber (Joe) Swagger of Lillington; and eight great-grandchildren Kayla, Michael, Kari, Braedon, Kholten, Clayton, Ashlinn, and Mallory. Funeral services celebrating Zeno's life will be conducted 6:30 p.m. Thursday, December 13, 2012 at Woodland Baptist Church with Mike Groce, Joel Groce and Rev. Tim Gammons officiating.